M000093541

Dancing With Grace Amazing

COPYRIGHT © Dr. Danny Griffin,
1st Edition December 2018
Printed in the United States of America

Dr. Danny Griffin
dwadegriffin@gmail.com
www.SpiritualMaintenance.org

DEDICATION

I dedicate this book to the administration, teachers and staff of Hampden DuBose Academy in Zellwood, Florida whose faithfulness to education and God's Word impacted my life when I was 15 & 16 in 1952-1954. It was there GOD'S GRACE AMAZING captured my NEEDY life. Setting my spiritual compass on JESUS CHRIST, HIS CROSS and RESURRECTION, not religion. My JOURNEY would never be the same. So-Be-It

Table of Contents

INTRODUCTION

Solomon of old said,

> *"...my son, be warned; the writing of many books is endless, and excessive devotion to books is wearying to the body."* Ecclesiastes 12:12

In a world of mass communication of every kind the printed word is still king of the hill. Stores devoted to books of all kinds and description are to be found everywhere. Magazines and newspapers for every taste are plentiful. We are flooded with words and information of every kind. Yet many of us are still driven to address our world with more words and thoughts.

I stand at times in a bookstore filled with printed words of every description and in every form concerning every issue known to mankind, wondering why with all this available knowledge do we still repeat our same old patterns of prejudice and hate, war and injustice. Perhaps I write to understand better myself and my world. Perhaps it is a defense against the constant encroaching darkness of human inability. Maybe it comes from a desire to address my own pain within the human condition and define who I am.

I grew up and lived all of my life inside that which is called church. My father, grandfather and uncle were all active, properly trained ministers in a world where purpose and reason for life and living was bound up in human performance of a religious kind. Go to church, read the Bible, perform faithfully all the expected requirements of expressed faith and our ordered purpose in life would drive us to victory. Such performance seemed to work for those who sought formulas for a successful life of faith and from my understanding live, "a successful Christian life." Thus they arrived at a very ordered and controlled existence, waiting for eternity and its implied adventure with a God that supposedly set the basic formula in motion.

God, from my vantage point in life has never been boxed and from my point of view refuses to be controlled by schemes or formulas. The good news of the Gospel of Jesus Christ is not about do, go or be anything, but about done. His life for our life means we receive a gift beyond all explanation and over a lifetime that gift expands into wisdom and service unknown to human effort.

When humans set out to give direction and purpose to life and its meaning we can be assured of developing systems. Systems demand teachers and explainers who then demand pay and politics and then control ensues. "Grace defined" is the heart of a man filled with contradictions, setbacks and unfulfilled dreams, just as is all mankind.

Grace comes to us in the midst of our inability and failures. Grace is a power outside human determination and purpose and comes to each of us as an undeserved gift, not of ourselves. Grace is the ultimate power that God has chosen to give life for death, hope for failure, good for evil and virtue for depravity. Grace is that great and precious provision against the background of darkness and perversion. Grace and grace alone has the power to save, keep, heal and bless amidst all the dirt and grime of life's nitty-gritty.

The hope of the whole world is not religions and philosophies but in the "power of God unto salvation to everyone who believes." (Romans 1:16) God defined His "Grace upon Grace" in the person of Jesus Christ. (John 1) The power driven life is found in the face of Jesus Christ and it is all about Him, not us. (2 Corinthians 4:5-7)

Come to this wonderful "power" by "grace through faith," not of yourselves. This power will drive your life now and for eternity being sufficient amidst life's good, bad and ugly. We are designed, bought and paid for by God Himself. You are invited to trust God and receive the gift of His righteousness manifest in Jesus Christ through His love and grace by faith!

Danny Griffin

Charlotte, NC

FOREWORD

This book is written for thought and discussion. For its layout the acrostic is used as the force of each chapter. The word "**GRACE**" is the heartbeat of each one as it applies itself to each part of our lives. The defining of grace in all its beauty is as impossible as it is to capture the beauty of a sunrise with all its dimensions on a canvas. One can respond in a subjective manner with all the emotion of the moment and even repeat it again and again but never absorb all that it is. Thus each chapter takes a small breath from the awesomeness of God's nature and character revealed in His **GRACE.** Inhaling the moment gives us great hope and encouragement in good times and bad to God's glory and our good. Take a deep breath and inhale His power and glory. Let us therefore come boldly unto the throne of **GRACE** that we may obtain mercy, and find **GRACE** to help in time of **NEED**. (Hebrew 4:16.

But my God shall supply all your **NEED** according to his riches in glory by Christ Jesus. (Philippians 4:19)

AMAZING GRACE HOW SWEET IT IS!

Amazing grace how sweet the sound

That saved a wretch like me

I once was lost but now am found

Was blind but now I see!

Twas Grace that taught my heart to fear

And Grace my fears relieved

How precious did that Grace appear

The hour I first believed!

-John Newton-

The Nature of Grace

Grace is God acting freely, according to His own nature as Love with no promises or obligations to fulfill and act righteously in view of the cross.

Grace therefore is uncaused in the one who receives. Its cause lies completely in the GIVER, in GOD.

Grace is absolutely the final authority. It is sovereign, not having debts to pay or fulfilled conditions on our part to wait for. It can act toward whom and how it pleases. It can, and often does, place the worst sinner in the highest favor.

Grace cannot act where there is a thought of either deserving or ability. Grace is not giving help but is absolute. It does all.

There being no cause in the creature why Grace should be shown, the creature must be bought off from trying to give reason to God for His Grace.

The discovery by the creature that he is truly the object of divine Grace works the greatest humility. The receiver of Grace is brought to know his/her own absolute unworthiness and his complete inability to attain worthiness. He finds himself/herself blessed because of God's determination, a principle of Grace outside himself/herself.

Therefore flesh has no place in the plan of Grace. This is the reason why Grace is often hated or rejected by the proud, natural mind of mankind. For this very reason the true believer rejoices! For he/she knows that in him/her, that is in the flesh, is no good thing. He finds God glad to bless him/her just as he/she is! This is truly AMAZING GRACE!

Proper Attitude Under Grace

To believe and to consent to be loved while a sinner and unworthy, is the great secret of God's Grace

To refuse to make "resolutions and vows" for that is to trust in the flesh

To expect to be blessed though realizing more and more our lack of worth

To testify and declare God's goodness at all times

To be certain of God's future favor and blessing yet to be sensitive and tender of conscience toward Him

A man/woman under Grace begins to have more burdens for others than for themselves.

Things We Under Grace Discover

To "hope to be better" is to fail to see yourself "in Christ only"!

To be disappointed with yourself is to have believed in yourself instead of God and His Grace.

To be discouraged is unbelief as to God's purpose and plan of blessing for you.

To be proud is to be blind! We have no standing before God in ourselves.

The lack of God's blessing comes from unbelief not from failure of devotion.

Real devotion to God arises not from man's will to show it, but from the discovery that blessing has been received from God while we were still unworthy and undevoted!

To declare devotion first and blessing second is to reverse God's order and proclaims Law, not Grace. The Law made man's blessing dependent on devotion. Grace gives unconditional, underserved blessing. Our devotion may follow, but does not always do so in proper measure and response to Grace!

Grace is Grace / It Stands Alone! A Gift!

GRACE IS NOT giving up anything to receive God's love!

GRACE IS NOT becoming good enough for God to love!

GRACE IS NOT doing religious works of any kind to receive God's love such as (joining churches / walking aisles / making religious decisions / water baptism / learning religious stuff / talking God talk /

being confirmed / giving our hearts to God / giving up our sins).

Our Place Under God

He has been accepted IN CHRIST, who is his/her standing!

He/she is not "on probation"!

As to one's past life, it does not exist before God. He/she died at the cross, and Christ is his/her life!

Grace once given, is not withdrawn, for God knows all the details of human sin and inability beforehand. His actions were independent of them.

The failure of devotion on the part of him/her does not cause the withdrawal of bestowed grace (as it would under the Law).

WILLIAM R. NEWELL

FROM HIS WONDERFUL BOOK / EXPOSITION OF ROMANS / I HEARD HIM SPEAK AS A STUDENT AT HAMPDEN DUBOSE ACADEMY IN 1953

DANCING WITH GRACE AMAZING OUTLINE

Birth / Life – Chapter One

G   God's

R   Righteousness

A   At

C   Christ's

E   Expense

Growth Life – Chapter Two

G   Give

R   Receive

A   Anothering

C   Conviction

E   Endurance

Body Life / Personal – Chapter Three

G   Gifts

R Rest

A Acknowledge

C Character

E Exalt

Body Life / Corporate – Chapter Four

G God's Word

R Renew

A Accountability

C Community

E Edify

Worship Life – Chapter Five

G Gloria

R Responsibility

A Attitude

C Confession

E Exalt

Witness Life – Chapter Six

G Generosity

R Reality

A Authenticity

C Confidence

E Encounter

World Life – Chapter Seven

G Guarded

R Redeemed

A Approved

C Consistent

E Evidence

Work Life – Chapter Eight

G Goals

R Repentance

A Ambition

C Conscience

E Excellence

Family Life – Chapter Nine

G Guidance

R Restore

A Availability

C Compassion

E Example

Study Life – Chapter Ten

G Graze

R Reason

A Access

C Context

E Examine

Prayer Life – Chapter Eleven

G Gratitude

R Responsive

A Address

C Commissioned

E Expectation

God's Life / Character – Chapter Twelve

G Grace And Truth

R Righteousness Our Cover

A Acquires Our Salvation

C Covenant Fulfilled

E Eternity In Our Hearts

Spirit Life – Chapter Thirteen

G Grows Us Up

R Redeems Us

A Acknowledges God's Gift

C Compels Us To Be Faithful

E Entreats All To Come To Him

Power Driven Life – Chapter Fourteen

G God's Work

R Righteousness Given

A Atonement Received

C Christ In Us

E Eternal Hope

Grace, the Power Driven Life!

Grace properly defined is not about our purpose but God's power alone which drives His purpose for our lives as believers as we grow in grace and knowledge. The power driven Life is about God's provision not our performance. It is not the purpose driven life!

G Gospel = God's good news salvation

R Righteousness = God's life in us

A Atonement = God's payment for sin

C Confidence = God's promises kept

E Established = God's security forever.

Grace Saves / Seals / Secures

Index

Chapter One

SPIRITUAL LIFE / NEW BIRTH LIFE

G God's
R Righteousness
A At
C Christ's
E Expense

> *"He [God] made Him [Christ] who knew no sin to be sin on our behalf that we might become the righteousness of God in Him [Christ]."* (2 Corinthians 5:21)

Salvation and spiritual birth is absolutely and completely a work of God, "not a human work, lest a person have a reason to boast." (Ephesians 2:8,9) It is indeed a gift of all gifts, "the gift of His righteousness." (Romans 5:17) The gift of righteousness is totally found in Jesus Christ. Thus God's righteousness is Jesus Christ himself.

When we receive Christ as our Saviour on the "basis of faith," we receive God's grace as salvation's power in our individual lives. "The just shall live by faith and we grow from faith to faith" in Christ and His grace, the by-product of the Gospel. (Romans 1:17) The

Gospel is the good news of Christ's death, burial and resurrection on our behalf. (I Corinthians 15:1-4)

We give God nothing in exchange for His grace. It is a gift, absolute and final. We don't give Him our life, our heart or our sins. We simply receive as full payment for all our sins past, present and future, our covering; just-if-ied never sinned. He takes our sins on Himself and gives us a spiritual birth, a new man inside our old bodies and natures which would never inherit the kingdom of God. (I Corinthians 15:50)

"Absent from the body, present with the Lord," is our new position in Christ. (2 Corinthians 5:8) This wonderful treasure of God's love and grace, the power of God for salvation, now indwells "our earthen vessel so that the glory be of God and not of ourselves." (2 Corinthians 4:7)

Jesus commanded us to,

> *"Seek first the kingdom of God and His righteousness and everything else would be added unto us."* (Matthew 6:33)

We are never commanded anywhere to give God our heart, walk an aisle, join a church, read our Bibles, know what the Bible teaches, be catechized, baptized or confirmed to receive the gift of His righteousness, our salvation.

The thief on the cross said,

> *"Remember me."* (Luke 23:42)

Jesus told Zacchaeus,

> *"I am going home to eat with you."* (Luke 19:5)

To the woman at the well Jesus said,

> *"I'll give you drink that will cause you to never thirst again."* (John 4:13-14)

To Nicodemus He said,

> *"You must be born again."* (John 3:7)

God gives and we receive the gift freely given and our response is not some long prayer or show of piety but "Thank you." For the rest of our life our response is "Thanks" and "Help." (John 3:16)

God's grace and our gratitude represent the eternal power of grace. Inside this receivership is the power to become all that God desires us to be. God is not to be found inside a formulistic box, nor are we. Inside His awesome sovereignty is that heart of grace that seeks out that one "lost sheep" that is outside the security of the fold. (Luke 15)

It is a truth indeed that God found us, not us Him, and all He asks of us is that we let Him love us. Those who do not receive His love are lost to His provision. Jesus did not come to bring damnation and condemnation but salvation. We all were already self-condemned because of our selfish and rebellious heart. (John 3:17-20)

To be lost, one must simply refuse to receive God's free gift of His righteousness which is mankind's covering freely offered, thus insulting His grace and denying His power. What we do and don't do is not the issue but what He has done on our behalf. We are not saved by our works but His only. It's not about us. It is about Him. We don't give or give up anything to receive this wonderful gift of salvation. We just receive the gift and give thanks.

God's grace brings spiritual birth and then spiritual power so that we can become all that He desires us to be. Growing in grace takes a lifetime of walking with the Father and the Son.

"He must increase and we must decrease." (John 3:30)

The Holy Spirit brings conviction, forgiveness, strength and healing to us in the war between the flesh and our old nature and our wonderful, new, eternal life. The power of grace manifests itself as we learn not to fight the old dying nature and its rebellion and instead feed the precious, new nature God has given us in Christ. Pray that we will all discover "the power driven life" again and again as we "grow in the grace and knowledge of our Lord and Saviour Jesus Christ," remembering always that, "To Him be the glory, both now and to the day of eternity." Amen! (2 Peter 3:18)

Chapter Two

GROWTH LIFE / DISCIPLESHIP

G Give

R Receive

A Anothering

C Conviction

E Endurance

The Grace to GIVE

Once I choose to allow God to love me, forgive all my sins and give me the gift of His righteousness I am ready to discover a totally new power available to my life. Whether we speak of it as being saved, born again, trusting in Christ or giving our heart to God, it declares that He offered a gift of love and we received Him, trusted Him or believed Him for salvation.

We may have been in a bar, at home, in the forest, by a lake, walking on a beach, in a church, in a vehicle, in a church building, at daytime or night, we could receive this gift wherever and whenever our inner man heard the message. Regeneration is an absolute work of God. He gives and we receive.

As our heart responds to the first awareness of His entering our space there is a desire to give to someone else that sense of wonder and peace that we cannot explain but desire to express or manifest it's reality by sharing with another human. The impulse to share the unexplainable drives us for the rest of our lives, sometimes more intense than at others. A gift given out of love cries out to be returned.

Paul the Apostle says,

> *"We were created in Christ Jesus unto good works which God ordained that we walk in them."* (Ephesians 2:10)

His work on our behalf empowers us to reach beyond ourselves.

Paul says it again like this,

> *"Be careful to maintain good works, for these are good and profitable unto men."* (Titus 3:8-9)

None of our works are to merit God's free gift, but because of His gracious love and grace on our behalf we now "in Christ" can live a life of giving to others as we learn to live a life "driven by grace's power." His power is out of His overflow in us. "Christ is the hope of glory." (Colossians 1:27)

The Grace to RECEIVE

Perhaps the most difficult part of the message of Grace and God's love and forgiveness is our inability to receive such a marvelous truth. Guilt is a strange emotion that can cause us not to believe that God can love us completely and forgive us absolutely. The matter of being worthy of such love confronts us. Life experiences have proved again and again that no one in this life truly forgives and forgets setting us free from our bondage, whatever it is.

Religion has confronted the world more with guilt and expectations than love and forgiveness. The first reaction of mankind because of conscious and unconscious religious conditioning, based on performance is to not believe the gospel of grace and truth.

To forgive others is often more easily done than to forgive ourselves. God's grace providing love and forgiveness is often rejected because we do not feel worthy or qualified and surely it cannot be true. We must never base God's forgiveness on human feeling and experience, but rather on that which we know based on Scripture concerning God's nature and character. God only wants us to allow Him to Love us!

"For God so loved the world that He gave His one of a kind Son, that whosoever believeth in Him [receives His gift of Himself] should not perish but have everlasting life." (John 3:16)

We must be empowered by God's grace to receive "the gift of His righteousness." (Romans 5:17) Thus receiving is a work of the Holy Spirit in our lives as we understand that He not only forgives, but qualifies us to stand approved and receive His grace. (Colossians 1:12)

ANOTHERING by Grace

Jesus said,

"They will know that you are my disciples if you have love for one another." (John 13:35)

"Love one another even as I love you." (John 13:34)

The writer of Hebrews said,

"Let us consider how to stimulate one another to love and good deeds."

Anothering thus is a way of manifesting our love and grace toward others in a way that will bring encouragement and "bear one another's burdens", thus fulfilling the law of Christ." (Galatians 6:2)

Anothering is not in the dictionary and is not an acknowledged word but it expresses well what "another" is all about. It is a work of the Holy Spirit and not a self-developed skill. It operates from the inside out as we grow in grace over a lifetime. We make a choice to another based on truth not an emotion or feeling that must be developed. It is truly a work of God through His grace teaching us to practice the "power driven life."

The CONVICTION of Grace

Paul the Apostle spoke with conviction when he declared,

> *"...I know whom I have believed and I am convinced that He is able to guard what I have entrusted to Him until that day."* (2 Timothy 1:12)

The growth of each of us believer/disciples happens as we internalize God's truth and learn to apply it to our daily walk. This is a lifetime pursuit. Maturity comes slowly building upon the authority of God's Word in our lives over a lifetime. Knowledge has a tendency to give us the big head and make us proud of our spiritual progress and humility.

Wisdom comes slowly and mixed with life experience and humility makes for strong character and convictions that manifest grace and truth served with love and patience. Convictions and grace are applied over time keeping us from being legalistic and demanding. Loving and anothering, always remembering how much God's grace has been shown to us helps us keep our balance and focus.

Because of life's unpredictability, we over a lifetime must allow the Holy Spirit to daily fine tune our lives and attitude as we practice allowing the fruit of the Spirit to operate in our lives. (Galatians 5:22-23) Because we are human, fragile and very easily shaken by life's circumstances and difficulties we may not always hold the line on our convictions and expectations perfectly.

We here must walk by faith with great grace and humility, acknowledging our sins before God and our faults one to another so as to,

> *"walk in the light as He is in the light, knowing that the blood of Jesus Christ cleans us from all sin." (I John 1:7, 9)*

No matter what our convictions are, they must always be bound in love and shared with grace, "knowing that He that began a good work in us will finish it." (Philippians 1:6)

Our convictions must never grow rigid and mean but strong and loving, expressing themselves in our faithful walk, restoring the distracted and fallen with patience as we discover daily "the power driven life."

The ENDURANCE of Grace

The writer of Hebrews again speaks as we are challenged to,

> "...run with endurance the race that is set before us."
> (Hebrews 12:1)

Endurance is life on the long term not an instant, quick fix. In our world of instant everything we have taken the most vital of human experiences and surrendered it to polls, consumerism, user friendly philosophy and entertaining sound bites.

None of this produces endurance in our character nor patience in our daily walk. Sermons and performance of any kind do not disciple people. People disciple people and grace with power is manifested in the one on one, up close and personal relationship.

Our lives change because we walk with someone who walks with Christ. Attendance at meeting, great music and sermons may offer some insight and inspiration but where we learn to follow Christ is in the daily grind in the real world, among real people and real sinners.

Discipleship's bottom line is availability and endurance. Up close and personal discipleship demands first of all availability to another and then endurance of both the pain and pleasure of walking together. Our greatest joy in our walk of "grace through faith" is bearing a brother/sister's burden, and this will call for much prayer, patience and caring over the long haul.

When all the piety is stripped away and the mask is off then endurance becomes a reality to the one who really cares. It has been said by wiser that I that one does not really care at all for a brother/sister in Christ until he/she bears their pain and hurt.

Even ground work for sharing the Gospel in another's life demands touching their space with grace and compassion. Their coming to respond to God's wonderful gift of love and forgiveness will depend on our faithfulness to love through all the good, bad and ugly of the human process.

Life is tough and we must never play to the grandstand but rather be as invisible as possible so as to allow that person to trust, finding us available when needed. Endurance never means control or breaching a trust.

The power of grace in endurance is leaning to fulfill the command of Paul who said,

> *"Make it your ambition to live a quiet life, mind your own business and work with your hands then both other believers and unbelievers will be blessed."* (I Thessalonians 4:9-12)

No place is grace's power more witnessed than in the process of endurance both with ourselves and others. God, who is longsuffering and patient with us as we grow and go, teaches us that the "power driven life" is filled with graceful endurance. (Ephesians 3:20-21)

Chapter Three

BODY LIFE / INNER MAN

G Gifts

R Rest

A Acknowledge

C Character

E Exalt

The moment I believe the good news of God's love and forgiveness Paul said,

> "...by one Spirit we were all baptized into one body." (I Corinthians 12:13)

God's grace applied to my life empowers me to receive all His provisions and promises. The body of Christ is composed of all believers worldwide, thus "the body is not one but many." (I Corinthians 12:14) Each believer stands before God individually yet also joined corporately to every other believer by God's love and grace.

Our growth in grace and spiritual power is a very individual matter over a lifetime, but we also are a great multitude corporately worldwide. God has ordained certain measures of growth for us. That in turn strengthens our development individually while glorifying Him and the body of believers universally.

Our individual growth should start immediately as the grace that birthed us grows us "in Christ." Each brings his own personality, conditioning, circumstances and choices to the walk of faith. Empowered by grace we learn over a lifetime to surrender piece by piece each part of all that we are, sometimes in very small installments, realizing that in our salvation He provided us with all that Christ is at one time.

We often dance three steps forward and two steps back but we do dance. We discover the need early to find others of like mind "in Christ" to grow with and walk with. We soon realize that growth is not always instant or easy as our "inner man" grows through stages of development as we confront real life and our "old nature" with all its baggage.

Individual and corporate spiritual growth will become a blessing to us and others as we claim the personal promise,

> "...that He would grant us according to the riches of His glory to be strengthened with power through His Spirit in the inner man." (Ephesians 3:16)

GIFTS / Grace's Overflow

The Greek word for grace and gift is rooted in the same word. The gifts of the Spirit are a manifestation of grace and its power. As ham is to gravy so grace is to gifts, from which spiritual essence flows. Thus "amazing grace," is that which is manifest in each believer as a special gift or gifts given to address lives and bless.

Every single believer must know from the moment of His receiving God's love and forgiveness that God has that special gift or gifts of grace's expression by which each believer's individual relationship with God might be expressed within the corporate body of Christ. Much is said about gifts, but it appears in my experience that so little is realized.

It should never be a matter of our self-inspection seeking to discover as it were some deep, mystical expression of grace. Rather, it is the joy of discovery in one's daily walk where gifts manifest and express themselves as they are authored and directed by the Holy Spirit. We should always seek to be natural in spiritual things and spiritual in natural things to God's glory and our good.

Pray daily in your intimate moments with God that He would reveal to you His place and power for you and in you each day. The gifts of the Spirit will flow as normal as breathing and all will be blessed. The power of grace in and through us will drive our lives with joy and peace. Practice brings rest in Him. (I Corinthians 12)

REST / Grace at Ease

Jesus Christ is the believer's rest. We struggle in our life of faith as we learn time and again that we must indeed rest "in Him." The "in Him" relationship is repeatedly spoken of in the epistles of the New Testament and we must learn to park there and never be moved. This too is a lifetime process of leaning and growing. Herein lays our rest.

The writer of Hebrews reminds us,

> *"Let us therefore be diligent to enter into that rest, For the one who has entered His rest has himself also rested from his/her works."* (Hebrews 4:9-11)

In the natural we spell rest,

Restless
Energy
Standing
Tough

God desires us to spell rest,

Relax
Enjoy
Saviour's
Triumph

Grace applied to our daily struggle will teach us that Christ alone can turn our momentary stress to rest. Feelings and emotions will fail us. Self-fixing and hand wringing will only multiply our pain and hurt. As one sits down in our favorite chair to rest ourselves, we must dare sit down upon God's precious promises and provisions. Remember His track record. He has never failed or forsaken us.

Paul the Apostle clearly commanded us to,

> *"Be anxious for nothing but in everything with prayer and supplication with thanksgiving let your request be made known to God."* (Philippians 4:6)

Walking in the Spirit in all things is a lifetime pursuit and we must be reminded of this matter every waking moment.

The writer of Hebrews declared,

> *"...for the mature because of practice have their senses trained to discern good and evil."* (Hebrews 5:14)

This reality can be applied to every detail in our faith pilgrimage over a lifetime. Because of the human condition inside our "old sin nature" it is easier to speak of rest than to "rest indeed." The power driven life learns to drink from grace's fountain moment by moment daily "on the basis of faith."

ACKNOWLEDGE / The Mind of Grace

Solomon of old spoke great truth when he exhorted us,

> "Trust in the Lord with all your heart and do not lean on your own understanding. In all your ways acknowledge Him, and He will make your paths straight." (Proverbs 3:5-6)

Acknowledging God in our daily walk is not based on piety, posturing and pretense but a genuine awareness that our flesh nature contains the memory of all that we have done and all that we have become to this present moment. Thus the grace factor in our lives calls us to routinely remind ourselves that the power of our "life in Christ" is the "mind of Christ" that is ours to draw from by faith.

We are told that "The just shall live by faith, for in it the righteousness of God is revealed from faith to faith". (Romans 1:17) Thus to acknowledge God is to agree with His life, His grace, His forgiveness and His provision on our behalf and allowing absolutely nothing to stand in the way of its application to our personal, daily walk. Not even our sins and inability.

Much as the basketball player fouls, acknowledging his/her foul before the game continues, we must also acknowledge our particular sin that breaks fellowship not relationship. This is not ever to be thought of as penitence, a work, guilt trip or performance, but rather in a moment of time acknowledging that you fouled, stumbled, messed up, wiped out and in essence "came short of the glory of God."

Indeed sin is just that, a missing of the mark. Agreeing with God is not guilt tripping or groveling, nor is it pretending it never happened, but believing that He is who He said He is and He did on our behalf what He said He did. We were already completely forgiven of all our sins past, present and future in His death, burial and resurrection. Drawing from that reality we are restored to the power of forgiveness. (I John 1:9)

In a moment of time our agreeing with His provision restores all fellowship instantly as we live out in the flesh the consequence of our sin, which calls us to desire it never again. "But if we do sin, we do have our mediator, advocate, and go between, without fail as He promised." (I John 2:1-2)

Grace's power is the only truth that can drive our life. All other powers offer only temporary relief and improvised formulas that ultimately fail. Forever and always, day in and day out, in the good and bad of life, we must "in all our ways acknowledge Him."

CHARACTER / Grace's Roadmap

Character reveals who we really are when no one is looking. Personality is the way others see us. God knows all that we are and are not and loves us unconditionally. He hates our sin and all the evil of the heart but He loves the sinner with redeeming love.

Jesus said,

"He came to seek and to save that which is lost."

We are included and we fit the label "sinner" which means we have "come short of the glory of God" thus in street terms, lost and undone. Over a lifetime once we trust His forgiveness and grace God begins to paint on the canvas of our lives a picture of many colors, forms and strokes as we allow. Often the canvas is filled with our own strokes and forms and thus some parts of our picture reveal self-will and erratic adaptations that besmirch and disfigure the painting of our life.

The life picture is our character and God knows it well but to those of us He knows as His, He views it all with grace, allowing our stupidity and inability to become a part of our canvas allowing us to "hit the wall." In our failure as His child we turn back to the Father time and again as He teaches us through our pain and hurt. Proven character doesn't just happen but is the by-product of tribulations and perseverance and Scriptures declare that proven character produces hope.

The character defined by grace reveals many flaws, warts and distortions but also reveals God's refining work as He teaches us through it all. We can adjust our personality to the given moment or occasion but not so our character. When our life canvas is finished in this dimension, God who knows the heart and our standing before Him will take pride in our canvases. No matter how tainted and lacking, each canvas that was trusted to His care will be signed by none other than Jesus Christ the Righteous.

As we honor the scribblings of our own human children, some better than others but belonging to our children, we showcase them all with equality before the world. So the God of heaven and earth having chosen to love broken, damaged people gives us who trust the gift of His Righteousness, a place of great blessing, not because of "works we have done" but according to His mercy our canvas stands "approved by Jesus Christ."

Thus our character is the sum total of all that we are and will sooner or later surface to reveal who we truly are. Whereas our personality can be managed and cover the true self. Our world is oriented around personality and performance, but God looks on the heart and knows all the details of our character and loves us, seeking to produce in us a reflection of His love and grace.

As God even uses things intended for evil, for good, let us pray that our character will grow stronger and we will draw others to God's grace at work in and through us as

> "...we work out our salvation with fear and trembling, for it is God who works in us to will and to do His good pleasure." (Philippians 2:12-13)

Then and only then will our personality flow from our character and we will become more authentic in all that we do and say.

Our personality will then begin to reflect the reality of who we are and our character will keep us anchored to the solid rock of God's faithfulness to love us and be our strength and wisdom. We will stand apart from our culture and world order refusing to allow the shallowness of a managed image, reflected in our personality, based on our flesh and its desires and agendas. This is a lifelong process and only inside a grace driven life will we again and again discover real life and its meaning and power.

EXALT / Grace's Reward

The great power of grace in our personal walk pays many dividends; the greatest of all is God being honored in our bodies of flesh and our life of faith.

The Apostle Paul said of himself,

> "…according to my earnest expectation and hope, that I shall not be put to shame in anything, but that with all boldness Christ shall even now, as always, be exalted in my body whether by life or by death." (Philippians 1:20)

Again we must remember that this is not an instant reality, but a lifetime adventure. Leaning and discovering not only how precious God's grace is, but learning again and again that "…the heart is desperately wicked and deceitful above all else." (Jeremiah 17:9) and "the flesh sets its desire against the Spirit and the Spirit against the flesh." (Galatians 2:17) The path to exaltation of Christ in our lives is servanthood.

Jesus declares,

> *"...the greatest among you shall be your servant. And whoever exalts himself shall by humbled and whoever humbles himself shall be exalted."* (Matthew 23:11,12)

Humility is the bottom line in our life of faith inside of grace's manifest power. We must never think of ourselves as super righteous and great doers of good. Thinking that God is privileged to have us on board His cause is foolish. It is God's righteousness, a gift that works in and through us as a conduit honoring Him. We don't work for God. He works in and through us to His glory and our good.

Jesus said the work of God, "...is believing Him who God sent." (John 6:29) Remember it is grace's gifts working in and through us and us resting in Him, acknowledging Him always as our source, our character reflecting His work in us over a lifetime as we grow in grace and knowledge and finally, His exaltation in and through all that we are. Grace is empowered and made real by our genuine humility.

James the brother of Jesus declared,

"Humble yourselves in the presence of the Lord and He will exalt you." (James 4:10)

The great joy of the grace driven life is that He is exalted in and through us and we in turn are exalted by Him.

Chapter Four

BODY LIFE / CORPORATE

G God's Word
R Renewal
A Accountability
C Community
E Edify

Corporate gathering is not essential for saving grace. Spiritual growth demands accountability with other believers.

We are commanded to,

> "… consider how to stimulate one another to love and good deeds by not forsaking our assembling together…encouraging one another so as to hold fast to our hope without wavering, for God is faithful…" (Hebrews 10:23-25)

We have called our gathering "going to church" which really fails to see the larger picture of "being the church" 24/7. Thus the Scripture, [God's Word] focuses our spiritual growth as a walk with others, denying us a "loner status" not in relationship to our personal salvation but our "spiritual growth" as we practice "anothering." (Romans 15:1-7, 13-14)

The Biblical meaning of church is a reference to believers who have been placed into the church which Christ loved and gave Himself on her behalf by the Holy Spirit the moment we believed. (I Corinthians 12:13 / Ephesians 5:22-33) The church is not a place but a people, set apart as temples of the Holy Spirit in a hurting, broken world.

GOD's Word

Jesus declared,

> *"Where two or three are gathered in His name there He is in their midst."* (Matthew 18:20)

When He appeared after the resurrection He shared concerning Himself from the Law of Moses and the Prophets and the Psalms that they must be fulfilled. He opened their minds to understanding the Scriptures. (Luke 24:44-49) Thus they were commanded to make sure they "handled accurately the Word of God and not wrangle about words to the ruin of the hearers." (2 Timothy 2:14-15)

The Word of God is declared to be,

> *"Living and active, sharper than a two edged sword piercing as far as the Soul and Spirit...able to judge the thoughts and intentions of the heart."* (Hebrews 4:12-13)

We should be as the Bereans who "searched the Scriptures daily to see if they were so." (Acts 17:11) The message of grace is the theme of salvation history from Genesis to Revelation. The New Testament is in the Old Testament contained and the Old Testament is in the New Testament explained. We must study both in context in order to discover God's will and way revealed in His grace and justice on behalf of all mankind.

RENEWAL

God's grace continually appealed to Israel on the basis of his covenant, design and love for her. The Old Testament prophets appealed continually for Israel to repent and experience revival. The Holy Spirit was not yet given to indwell those who believed God, but rather came upon persons for special service and leadership.

After the death of Jesus on the cross and His resurrection they tarried in the city of Jerusalem until the Holy Spirit sealed and endued them with power. Thus today as believers we are indwelt with the Holy Spirit and empowered to serve and give witness to Jesus Christ. The word for us is to,

> *"not be drunk with wine wherein is excess but be FILLED with the Spirit." (Ephesians 5:18)*

We are reminded "not to GRIEVE the Holy Spirit by which we are sealed for the day of redemption" and "not to QUENCH the Spirit." (Ephesians 4:30, I Thessalonians 5:19) We are thus commanded to be RENEWED in the spirit of your mind and put on the new self which in the likeness of God has been created in righteousness and holiness of the truth." (Ephesians 4:24-25)

Thus in finality we are reminded to "not be conformed to this world system but transformed by the RENEWING of our minds, proving what is the will of God, which is well pleasing to God therefore perfect." The revival of the Old Testament is the renewal of the New Testament and made manifest by "walking in the light as He is in the light having fellowship, [renewal/revival] and the blood of God's son Jesus cleanses us from all sin."

ACCOUNTABILITY

Jesus sent His disciples out two by two. The missionary work of the book of Acts often was done by two or more traveling together. There is a great need in the human makeup to have accountability with another by which we are encouraged and strengthened.

It is written of Paul the Apostle that,

> *"When he came into Macedonia his flesh had no rest and he was afflicted on every side with conflicts and fears within when God who comforts the depressed, comforted him by the coming of Titus."* (2 Corinthians 7:5-6)

Scripture declares,

> *"Bear one another's burdens and thus fulfill the law of Christ."* (Galatians 6:2)

Our lives are intricately bound up with each other brother and sister in Christ, and we need desperately to be accountable so as to share our weaknesses and strengths. (Galatians 6:1) Bottom line, it is good to be able to share intimately and trustingly with another believer before the Lord as we grow in grace, learning to walk and lean on the Holy Spirit in all areas of our journey.

COMMUNITY

There is no greater shelter from the world, the flesh and the devil than the grace community. Size and number, nickels and noses are never an issue. Gathering wherever you can in a home, café, market place or a quiet place and sharing God's Word, prayer and encouraging words of comfort and praise to God's glory and our good is true communion, thus common-unity.

We should remember always there where two or three are gathered, God is in their midst. (Matthew 18:20, Acts 2:43-47, Acts 4:32-35) Those who worship God must remember that we "worship in Spirit and truth." We are to be of the "same mind" and "one voice, glorifying God" as we accept one another as He accepted us. (Romans 15:4-7)

Jesus said,

> *"A new commandment I give you that you love one another and by this all men will know you are my disciples if and because you love one another."* (John 13:34-35)

Love is GRACE in shoe leather revealing true community.

EDIFICATION

Edification is the nurturing and sharing of both God's truth and our caring.

Scripture declares,

> *"We who are strong ought to bear the weaknesses of those without strength and not just please ourselves.*

Let each of us please our brother and sister in Christ for their own good to their edification. (Romans 15:1-3)

A vital part of edification is being admonished or encouraged to do that which is good and nurturing. (Romans 15:14)

Chapter Five

WORSHIP LIFE

G Glory
R Responsibility
A Attitude
C Confidence
E Exaltation

GLORY

"Whether then you eat or drink or whatever you do, DO ALL to the GLORY of GOD." (I Corinthians 10:31)

True worship is GRACE driven in every area of our lives. We have far too often compartmentalized worship making it a Sunday matter and a corporate, highly emotional operation by which we are worked up to a fever pitch so as to feel God and truly worship. True worship is worth-ship as we 24/7/365 practice the presence of God in every area of our lives with or without feeling.

Jesus declared,

"FATHER GLORIFY THY NAME." (John 12:28)

True worship answers this command daily. "For you have been bought with a price; therefore GLORIFY GOD IN YOUR BODY."

RESPONSIBILITY

A grace driven life is a life that consistently grows in grace and knowledge as we learn to "Respond to God's Ability." The life of the believer learns early on that he/she does not have the ability to live the life of faith within their own strength. Salvation is a work of God and working out our salvation must be a "faith dependency" on God's will and way in our lives daily. (Philippians 2:12-13)

The Scripture declares,

> "Now to Him who is ABLE to keep you from stumbling and to make you stand in the presence of His GLORY blameless with great joy to the only GOD OUR SAVIOUR through JESUS CHRIST our LORD be glory, majesty, dominion and authority before all time and now and forever. Amen" *(Jude 24-25)*

This is the heartbeat of our GRACE FILLED WORSHIP LIFE 24/7.

ATTITUDE

Attitude is an expression of our feelings toward a person or thing. A person with a bad or negative attitude is hard to deal with. A person with a positive attitude manifests confidence and care. In our relationship with God and His love and grace is a revelation of a different attitude. A grace empowered attitude is one of hope and joy even amidst the difficult and trying times. Thus it might be said to be a matter of the heart driven by a mind touched by God's grace and just not our human temperament or personality.

Scripture commands us as believers,

> *"Have the ATTITUDE in yourselves which was also in Christ Jesus...who emptied Himself and became in the likeness of man, taking on the mind of God becoming a bond servant. Thus He had the appearance of man; He humbled Himself being obedient to death on the cross. God bestowed on Him a name above every name, that all mankind should confess that Jesus Christ is Lord, to the Glory of God the Father."* (Philippians 2:1-11)

Thus Jesus Christ,

> *"the only begotten Son in the bosom of the Father, has explained Him." (John 1:18)*

CONFESSION

At the heart of true worship is confession that is "agreement with God that He is right." Thus private confession and public confession declares that God's love and grace allows us to proclaim before God and man that we have "missed the mark" in our lives as believers. Keeping short accounts with God allows His blessings to flourish in our lives and flow outward to others. (James 5:16, I John 1:9)

Scripture says,

> *"Don't sin, but if you do, you have an Advocate with the Father, Jesus Christ the righteous who is the satisfaction for our sins and the sins of the whole world."* (I John 2:1-3)

EXALTATION

Public worship is declared by David the psalmist that we should magnify the Lord and exalt His name together. (Psalm 34:3) Worship is not a performance art, but a total openness before God as our benefactor in all things. Thus our prayers and praise are driven by His nature and character which reveals Him as the Lord Most High over all the earth and exalted above all gods. (Psalms 97:9) Exaltations of thanksgiving flow from His name which represent His perfect faithfulness having worked wonders and plans formed long ago. (Isaiah 25:1) After Moses and Israel escaped the sea and Egypt they sang a great song and perfect example of praise and exultation to God for his deliverance.

> *"Then sang Moses and the children of Israel this song unto Jehovah and spake saying, I will sing unto Jehovah for He hath triumphed gloriously. The horse and his rider hath He thrown into the sea. Jehovah is my strength and song, and He is become my salvation. This is my God and I will praise Him, my father's God and I will exalt Him."* (Exodus 15)

JEHOVAH SHALL REIGN FOR EVER AND EVER!

Chapter Six

WITNESS LIFE

G Generosity

R Reality

A Authenticity

C Confidence

E Encounter

GENEROSITY

Grace is indeed the motor that gives and gives again and again. Another word for generosity is ABUNDANCE, more than enough.

The Scripture declares,

> *"...give and it shall be given unto you; good measure, pressed down, shaken together, running over shall they give into your bosom. For with what measure ye mete it shall be measured to you again."* (Luke 6:38)

Grace understood in its context always produces; not only gratitude but generosity which always blesses the true giver with an abundance in return of multiple blessings. Indeed we will reap what we sow in spiritual and material blessings by which we can once again be generous, "GRACE UPON GRACE"!

Generosity is one of the grandest and greatest points of witness in the world of human interaction. Mankind may argue with what you say, but can never debate love and grace in shoe leather. Giving puts us most in line with God's character.

> *"For God So Loved The World That He Gave..."!* (John 3:16)

REALITY

Paul the apostle lived in a real world and his witness manifested grace at every turn. He spoke of "becoming all things to all men that by some means he might win some." This demanded a listening and hearing of those other than himself that they might view his witness. He also demanded that we should love one another, mind our own business and work with our own hands so that it would be real with the unbeliever.

In another letter he declared that "we should conduct ourselves with wisdom with the unbeliever making most of our opportunity to witness. Again declaring that we should let our speech be seasoned with grace like seasoning with salt as we would our food, responding to each person's taste. (I Corinthians 9, I Thessalonians 4:9-12, Colossians 4:2-6) **GRACE HAS A TASTE THAT OTHERS MIGHT DESIRE!**

AUTHENTICITY

A few years ago I began carrying a small coin purse filled with broken pieces of pottery. They symbolize my brokenness, inability and insufficiency by which others can understand that true humility revealed by God's grace and forgiveness.

The Scriptures declare this principle,

> *"But we have this treasure in earthen vessels that the exceeding greatness of the power may be of God and not from ourselves."* (2 Corinthians 4:7)

Thus, our authenticity is best revealed when we are stripped of all self-righteousness and pride and we stand as imperfect, broken, greatly loved and forgiven who stand in God's grace and righteousness. Amazing Grace how sweet is the sound that saved the likes of you and me.

Paul the apostle declared that he was "chief of sinners," "least of the apostles" and finally "a nobody" and continued, "I am what I am by the GRACE of God." (I Timothy 1:12, I Corinthians 15:9-10, 2 Corinthians 12:11)

CONFIDENCE

Once our witness is set in those matters that anchor us to our Lord Jesus Christ then we build on the Word of God. Empowered by the Holy Spirit and prayer we can declare "that we worship in the Spirit of God and glory in Christ Jesus and put no confidence in the flesh."

We can declare,

> *"Being confident of this very thing that He that began a good work in us will perform it until He is finished." (Philippians 1:6, 3:3)*

Because of God's grace our witness is in His hand our confidence.

ENCOUNTER

The ultimate picture of our witness encounter is expressed clearly in the following Scripture.

RESPONSIBILITY:

> *"Continue steadfast in prayer, watching therein with thanksgiving, withal praying for us also."*

ACCOUNTABILITY:

"...that God may open unto us a door for the Word, to speak the mystery of Christ, that I may make it manifest as I ought to speak."

FLEXIBILITY:

"Walk in wisdom toward them that are without, redeeming the time. Let your speech be always with grace, seasoned with salt that ye may know how ye ought to answer each one." (Colossians 4:1-6)

Chapter Seven

WORLD LIFE

G Guarded

R Redeemed

A Approved

C Consistent

E Evidence

GUARDED

The world order is broken and we are commanded not to love the world; that is the lust of the flesh, the lust of the eyes and the pride of life. These are not from the Father, but the world order. (I John 2:15-16)

Jesus declared,

> *"If we gain the world but lose our soul what do we profit"?* (Luke 9:25)

Therefore we are commanded to,

> *"...and the peace of God which passes all understanding shall guard your hearts and minds in Christ Jesus." (Philippians 4:7)*

Grace must be removed from being defined by the world order but must always be defined by the unconditional love of God. Guard yourself always from those who would redefine grace and put it under law and control mankind with guilt instead of being set free by God's abundant GRACE upon GRACE. (John 1:14-18)

REDEEMED

Mankind's redemption comes on the basis of faith in the work of Jesus Christ on our behalf. Abraham believed God and it was counted for righteousness under the Old Covenant while under the New Covenant we are to believe God who as promised gave us His Son. Thus "Christ redeemed us from the curse of the Law having become a curse for us," so that the blessing of Abraham's covenant might come to us all. (Galatians 3:13-14)

Therefore when we believe God's work through Christ on our behalf, we would be sealed with the Holy Spirit of promise till the day of redemption. (Ephesians 1:13-14) In the world order this is the only redemption known to mankind approved and purchased by God.

APPROVED

In this fallen world order God has given us His living Word in the person of Jesus Christ. We have been given a written revelation of thousands of years written by many ordinary men who spoke by the Spirit of God those matters that came to pass in real time for our understanding of God's nature and character and mankind's rebellion and disobedience in the world order that He created. It became corrupted as did mankind.

This being so, under the New Covenant mankind was commanded to study the Word of God, rightly dividing it that we might be approved of God discovering the purpose of God for our lives. (2 Timothy 2:15) The Bereans searched the Scriptures with great eagerness to see whether they were so and in this broken world it is essential that we search the Scriptures for ourselves and not take others word for what is true and contained therein. (Acts 17:11)

CONSISTENT

As believers and receivers of grace our greatest growth and understanding should come through a consistent day by day searching of the Scriptures. We should seek answers to questions as we question answers, manifested by our steadfastness and persistence in our study of the Word. (I Corinthians 15:58)

EVIDENCE

In our study of the Word against the background of the world order we should seek truth and its evidence. Always remembering that the New Testament is in the Old Testament contained and the Old Testament is in the New Testament explained. Paul the Apostle's signature in the synagogues was that he "reasoned from the Scripture," that is the Old Testament, giving the evidence of Christ's suffering and the resurrection. Finally declaring that the Jesus he proclaimed was the "Christ." (Acts 17:1-3)

Chapter Eight

WORK LIFE

G Goals
R Repentance
A Ambition
C Conscience
E Excellence

GOALS

Grace is the ultimate power of the life of faith.

Paul the Apostle declared,

> *"I press on toward the GOAL for the prize of the upward call in Christ Jesus."*

That goal is the result of the power of the "abundance of grace, the gift of His righteousness" which empowers us with a response to God's-ability at work in us "the hope of glory." (Philippians 3:14, Romans 5:17, Colossians 1:27)

REPENTANCE

Jesus declared,

"The time is fulfilled and the kingdom of God is at hand: REPENT [change your mind] AND BELIEVE IN THE GOSPEL." (Mark 1:15)

Paul declared,

"...REPENT [change your mind] maintaining deeds in accord with REPENTANCE."

GRACE alone empowers us to repent in a broken world. It moves the roadblock of guilt and declares us righteous and receivers of God's grace setting us free from our great debt of sin.

Scripture declares that,

"God made Christ who knew no sin to be sin on our behalf that we might become the Righteousness of God in Christ." (2 Corinthians 5:21)

AMBITION

Our work life is our source of livelihood in the real world and as believers our greatest point of worship and witness to God's glory and our good. Ambitions as believers imply the spiritual energy to be credible and reveal integrity in our work to the glory of God. The Holy Spirit by magnifying God's grace in us and through us empowers us to be both salt and light in our daily life in the market place.

Scripture declares,

> "...make it your AMBITION to lead a quiet life and tend to your own business and work with your hands, just as we commanded you so that you may behave properly toward outsiders and not personally be in any need." (I Thessalonians 4:11-12)

We are commanded,

> "...whatever you do in word or deed do all in the name of the Lord Jesus, giving thanks through Him to God the Father."

CONSCIENCE

We as believers who have been GRACED by God are commended to, "Set aside Christ as Lord in your hearts, always being ready to make a defense to everyone who asks you to give an account for the hope that is in you with gentleness and respect, keeping a good CONSCIENCE so that in the thing you are falsely accused of your conduct in Christ may not be put to shame." (I Peter 3:15-16)

EXCELLENCE

Grace is the driving power of our life of faith daily and our greatest mission field is our daily work where

God's grace touches others more intently and is most observable.

> "Servants, obey in all things them that are your masters according to the flesh; not with eye-service as men pleasers, but in singleness of heart, fearing the Lord. Whatsoever you do, work heartily as unto the Lord and not unto men, knowing that from the Lord you shall receive the reward of your labor from the Lord Christ." *(Colossians 3:22-25)*

Chapter Nine

FAMILY LIFE

G Guidance

R Restore

A Availability

C Compassion

E Example

GUIDANCE

Everything comes with instructions or directions. The Scriptures have much to say about guidance from the Lord. Sermons, seminars and lectures cannot fix the family. Even love and nurture manifested with applied intimacy does not guarantee family unity and spiritual development.

The first children of Adam and Eve produced a murder. David the shepherd king had to deal with incest and rebellion in his children. I grew up as a pastor's son always hearing how bad "preachers' kids" are and their manifested problems. Yet caring, loving parents must not give up, but day in and day out offer love and care to each family member soaked in prayer.

The best guidance must be by example without being self-righteous and provoking the children to wrath by unrealistic expectations and rules. This is best practiced empowered by love and grace applied in great doses along with endless prayer and compassion.

RESTORE

Grace empowers family life to daily restore and rebound midst the process and stress of life's challenges. David of old prayed after his sinful activity of adultery and murder that God would "restore the joy of his salvation."

The prodigal son journeyed into a far country before he returned home to be restored with great joy. We are commanded to restore one who has sinned and fallen to a position of forgiveness and usefulness. It is here that grace paints the most beautiful pictures on the canvas of life.

AVAILABILITY

Availability within a family is an absolute essential quality. Out to lunch parents or children erode strength and confidence. For grace to operate in a family setting, individuals must see themselves as a single unit where each member seeks out the need of the other. Grace demands more of one another than rules and regulations.

COMPASSION

Grace is love and truth on fire expressed by compassion. It is a love that feels the hurt and pain of others. The powerful signature of grace reveals clearly the heartbeat of Jesus.

EXAMPLE

The power driven life is about grace in shoe leather, a lifestyle not a theory.

> *Let no man despise thy youth; but be thou an EXAMPLE of the believers, in word, in conversation, in charity, in spirit, in faith, in purity.* (I Timothy 4:12)

Chapter Ten

STUDY LIFE

G Grazing
R Reason
A Access
C Context
E Examine

GRAZING

Every person has their own style of Bible study and learning process. For my devotional reading I use the grazing approach reading from both the Old and New Testaments. I remember that the NEW TESTAMENT IS IN THE OLD CONTAINED AND THE OLD TESTAMENT IS IN THE NEW EXPLAINED.

Another principle I follow in my grazing process is what I refer to as the 20/20 RULE. That is a matter of context in reading the 20 verses before and after the verse I am reading. Another wonderful tool for grazing is the center reference column adding verses to each verse you are reading. Scriptures are the fuel for GRACE'S empowerment.

REASON

But sanctify the Lord God in your hearts: and be ready always to give an answer to every man that ask you a REASON of the hope that is in you with meekness and fear: (1 Peter 3:15)

ACCESS

GRACE calls out to the mind, heart and shoe leather of every believer demanding access for the purpose of growing in grace and knowledge.

CONTEXT

Context, context and context is one of the most important aspects of RIGHTLY DIVIDING THE WORD OF THUTH. Otherwise you prove most anything by taking any Scripture out of its context. God's Amazing Grace demands that we pay attention to the Biblical, Historical and Application context!

EXAMINE

"EXAMINE me, O Jehovah, and prove me; TEST my HEART and my MIND." (Psalm 26:2)

An unexamined life has little meaning, thus grace enables us to stand justified and guiltless before a holy God and examine ourselves daily to repent and confess our sins openly as we come boldly to the THRONE OF GRACE.

Chapter Eleven

PRAYER LIFE

G Gratitude

R Responsive

A Address

C Commissioned

E Expectation

GRATITUDE

"In nothing be anxious; but in everything by PRAYER and supplication with THANKSGIVING let your requests be made known unto God." (Philippians 4:6)

The heartbeat of PRAYER is gratitude and thanksgiving and from it flows all of God's promises and provisions called GRACE.

"Grace to you and peace be multiplied in the knowledge of God and of Jesus our Lord; seeing that His divine power hath granted unto us all things that pertain unto life and godliness through the knowledge of Him that called us by His own glory and virtue whereby he hath granted unto us his precious and exceeding great promises." (I Peter 1:3-4)

"...in everything give THANKS, for this is the will of God in Christ Jesus for you all." (I Thessalonians 5:18)

RESPONSIVE

"...the Spirit helps our infirmity; for we know not how to PRAY as we ought, but the Spirit himself makes intercessions for us with groanings which cannot be uttered and he that searches the hearts and knows what is the mind of the Spirit because He makes intercession for the saints according to the will of God. And we know that to those that love God all things work together for good, for them that are called according to HIS purpose." (Romans 8:26-28)

ADDRESS

"Grace to you and peace from God our Father and the Lord Jesus Christ. (Ephesians 1:2-3)

"Now the God of peace, who brought again from the dead the great shepherd of the sheep with the blood of an eternal covenant, our Lord Jesus, make you perfect in every good thing to do His will, working in us that which is well-pleasing in his sight THROUGH JESUS CHRIST; to whom be the glory for ever and ever Amen." (Hebrews 13:20)

GOD'S ADDRESS IS DIRECT THROUGH JESUS CHRIST!

"Having then a great high priest who has passed through the heavens, Jesus the Son of God, let us hold fast our confession. For we have not a high priest that

cannot be touched with the feeling of our infirmities; but one that has been in all points tempted yet without sin. Let us therefore draw near with boldness unto the THRONE OF GRACE, that we may receive mercy and may find grace to help in time of need." (Hebrews 4:14-16)

COMMISSIONED

"Pray without ceasing. In everything give thanks, for this is the will of God in Christ Jesus concerning you." (I Thessalonians 5:17-18)

EXPECTATION

"...I am not ashamed, for I know Him whom I have believed; I am persuaded that HE is able to guard that which I have committed unto HIM against that day." (2 Timothy 1:12)

Jesus declared,

"...when you pray, GO INTO YOUR CLOSET and close the door and pray to your Father who is in secret, and your Father who sees what is done in secret will reward you." (Matthew 6:6)

Scripture declares,

"...the Spirit helps our weakness, for we do not know how to pray as we should but the Spirit Himself

*intercedes for us with groanings too deep for words…"
(Romans 8:26)*

"Pray without ceasing." (I Thessalonians 5:17)

Jesus Christ came to seek and find us while we were yet sinners, dead in trespasses and sin. He came to die for us, to live in us and to use us for His glory and our good. In a world of talking heads and faceless crowds, the world of religion has become a consumer item. Its leadership has often become CEO minded rather than servant driven.

The life of faith is one of "Closet Power" and "Christ in us the hope of glory." The world of religion often develops a cosmetic, plastic piety, overdosed on meeting attending and sermon sampling. Jesus Christ came to reveal God's love for all mankind without partiality. He came to seek and to save the lost, least and lonely offering His righteousness as a gift of love and grace.

His death, burial and resurrection are the heart of the gospel of grace. He calls us to a life of humility and "Closet Power"! Jesus did not come to start a mass movement or win the world to Himself by corporate gimmicks and appeals. God throughout human history chose to use His power in one man or woman to address the world. Masses have indeed come to the simple message of the cross and resurrection, but discipleship demands a walk, up-close and personal. Jesus Christ always attached Himself to individuals revealing Himself in such a way that each human encounter built a personal relationship.

We are never commanded to go to church, but instructed in how to be the church. The true symbol of Jesus was the towel and the wash basin as He washed the feet of His disciples exampling the true servant.

Jesus declared,

> *"He that is the greatest among you is servant of all."* *(Matthew 23:11)*
>
> *"They will know that you are my disciples because you love one another." (John 13:35)*

Anothering is the application of "agape love" that is unconditional love that reaches out to the brokenness of believer and unbeliever alike until they are drawn to the Father. It is only through "Closet Power" that this kind of force and usefulness is constant. There is a need to come out of our quiet time with Jesus to serve others in His name.

Christianity and its many differing beliefs and dogmas often prove a turn off. When we follow Jesus in the Scriptures we discover a different Jesus.

Paul declared,

> "We should make it our ambition to live a quiet life, mind our own business and work with our hands." (I Thessalonians 4:11)

> "Sanctify the Lord in our hearts and be ready to give a reason of our hope to THOSE WHO ASK…"! (I Peter 3:15)

> "THUS BEING CAREFUL TO MAINTAIN GOOD WORKS, FOR THEY ARE GOOD AND PROFITABLE FOR MANKIND. LETTING OUR LIGHT SO SHINE AMONG MANKIND THAT THEY WILL SEE OUR GOOD WORKS AND GLORIFY OUR FATHER WHICH IS IN HEAVEN." (Matthew 5:16)

Chapter Twelve

GOD LIFE / SPIRITUAL WARFARE

G Graceless Journey

R Riotous Living

A Afflictions Abound

C Covenant Reviewed

E Eternal Signature

GRACELESS JOURNEY

"And the younger of them said to his father, 'Father, give me the portion of goods that comes to me'. And he divided unto them his living. And not many days after the younger son gathered all together and took his journey into a far country." (Luke 15:12-13)

RIOTOUS LIVING

"...there wasted his substance with riotous living. And when he had spent all, there arose a mighty famine in that land; and he began to be in want. And he went and joined himself to a citizen of that country and he sent him into his fields to feed swine." (Luke 15:13-15)

AFFLICTIONS ABOUND

"And he would fain have filled his belly with the husks that the swine did eat and no man gave unto him. And

when he came to himself, he said, 'How many hired servants of my fathers have bread enough and to spare and I perish with hunger'"! (Luke 15:16-17)

COVENANT REVIEWED

"I will arise and go to my father, and will say unto him, Father, I have sinned against heaven and before thee and am no more worthy to be called thy son; make me as one of thy hired servants." (Luke 15:18-19)

ETERNAL SIGNATURE

"And he arose and came to his father. But when he was yet a great way off, his father saw him and had compassion and ran and fell on his neck and kissed him. And the son said unto him 'Father, I have sinned against heaven and in thy sight and am no more worthy to be called thy son.' But the father said to his servants, 'bring forth the best robe and put it on him and put a ring on his hand and shoes on his feet. And bring forth the fatted calf and kill it and let us eat and be merry. For this my son was dead, and is alive again, he was lost and is found.' And they began to be merry." (Luke 15:20-24)

DADDY! I HURT:

"...you have received a spirit of adoption as sons by which we cry out, ABBA! FATHER! [DADDY]"! (Romans 8:15)

He (Jesus) was saying, "ABBA! FATHER [DADDY]"! God sent forth His Son, born of a woman, born under the Law so that He might redeem those who were under the Law that we might receive the adoption as sons. Because we as believers are His children, God has sent forth the Spirit of His Son into our hearts and we cry, "ABBA! FATHER! [DADDY]."

The words "Abba! Father!" is an Aramaic expression of endearment and may be translated daddy. JESUS CHRIST WAS BORN IN POVERTY; DIED IN PAIN, AGONY AND DISGRACE ON THE CROSS FOR ALL OUR SIN DEBT, LOVE'S FREE GIFT! So much of my spiritual growth has come through the struggle with bad choices, missed opportunities, confused thinking, thoughtlessness, selfishness and my old sin nature.

Philip Yancey in his wonderful book, WHERE IS GOD WHEN IT HURTS has listed some things that reveal positive realities to suffering which involve hurt and pain.

"Suffering is the great equalizer, common to all. Suffering produces dependence on God and for those that are healthy an interdependence on one another. Suffering causes us not to find our security in things that may soon be taken away. Suffering humbles the proud. Suffering causes cooperation not competition. Suffering

helps us distinguish necessities from luxuries. Suffering teaches patience born of dependence. Suffering helps us distinguish valid fears from exaggerated fears. Suffering gets our attention and causes us to listen with our inner ears, addresses our inner man."

Suffering or affliction as it is often called in the Scriptures gives us the ability to help others in their affliction. When a parent has to deal with the hurt and pain of a child, he often hears the cry, "DADDY! IT HURTS!" and instantly seeks the remedy for the pain. As believers we know that God is indeed touched by our infirmities.

Joseph said to his brothers,

"You meant evil against me, but God meant it for good."
(Genesis 50:20)

Thus situations, difficulties and failures at a moment in time may create hurt, pain and suffering but eventually produce blessing and spiritual growth.

Scripture declares,

"GOD CAUSES ALL THINGS TO WORK TOGETHER FOR GOOD TO THOSE WHO LOVE GOD, TO THOSE WHO ARE CALLED ACCODING TO HIS PURPOSE."
(Romans 8:28)

God's love and grace is manifest in Jesus Christ so that we can have peace in our inner man. Though HURT and PAIN are never pleasant, they can produce in us spiritual and emotional growth. Sin in the life of the believer also brings PAIN and HURT but with confession, fellowship and joy is restored. WE LIVE IN A BROKEN WORLD FILLED WITH ALL MANNER OF HURT AND PAIN. MAY WE PRAY DAILY THAT WE CAN LEARN TO BEAR ONE ANOTHER'S BURDEN AND FULFILL THE LAW OF CHRIST. IT'S CALLED ANOTHERING! JESUS BORE OUR SIN SO WE NOW BY HIS POWER BEAR THE BURDENS OF OTHERS!

Chapter Thirteen

SPIRIT LIFE

G Grows Us Up
R Redeems Us
A Acknowledges God's Gift
C Compels Us To Be Faithful
E Entreats All To Come

GROWS US UP

"As newborn babes, desire the sincere milk of the Word that ye may grow thereby." (I Peter 2:2)

"...But speaking the truth in love, may grow up in Him in all things which is the head, even Christ." (Ephesians 4:15)

"But grow in grace and in the knowledge of our Lord and Saviour Jesus Christ. To him be glory both now and forever. Amen" (2 Peter 3:18)

REDEEMS US

"Looking for that blessed hope and the glorious appearing of the great God and our Saviour Jesus Christ; who gave himself for us that he might redeem us from all iniquity and purify unto himself a peculiar people, zealous of good works." (Titus 2:13-14)

ACKNOWLEDGES GOD'S GIFT

"For by grace are ye saved through faith; and that not of yourselves it is the GIFT OF GOD, not of works lest any man should boast. (Ephesians 2:8-9)

"But not as the offence so also is the FREE GIFT. For if through the offence of one many be dead, much more the grace of God and the GIFT BY GRACE which is by one man, Jesus Christ hath abounded unto many. And not as it was by one that sinned, so is the GIFT; for the judgement was by one to condemnation but the FREE Gift is of many offences unto justification. For if by one man's offence death reigned by one; much more they which receive abundance of grace and of the GIFT OF RIGHTEOUSNESS shall reign in life by one, Jesus Christ. Therefore as by the offence of one judgment came upon all men to condemnation, even so by the righteousness of one the FREE GIFT came upon all men unto justification of life." (Romans 5:15-18)

COMPELS FAITHFULNESS

"O Lord, thou art my God; I will exalt thee, I will praise thy name for you have done wonderful things; your counsels of old are FAITHFULNESS AND TRUTH." (Isaiah 25:1)

"I will even betroth thee unto me in FAITHFULNESS, AND YOU SHALL KNOW THE LORD. (Hosea 2:20)

ENTREATS ALL TO COME

"That in the ages to COME He might shew the exceeding riches of His grace in His kindness toward us through Christ Jesus." (Ephesians 2:7)

"Till we all COME in the unity of the faith and of the knowledge of the Son of God, unto a perfect man, unto the measure of the stature of the fullness of Christ." (Ephesians 4:13)

"Let us therefore COME BOLDLY unto the throne of grace that we may obtain mercy and find grace to help in time of need." (Hebrews 4:16)

"The Lord is not slack concerning His promise, as some men count slackness; but is longsuffering to us-ward not willing that any should perish but that all should COME to repentance." (II Peter 3:9)

Repentance is a willingness to admit failure or sinfulness, brokenness, not a one-time act but a daily renewal and declaration. Daily we must be willing to be "broken and spilled out" to God's glory and our good.

This song says it beautifully,

One day a plain village woman
Driven by love for her Lord
Recklessly poured out a valuable essence

Disregarding the scorn
And once it was broken and spilled out
A fragrance filled all the room
Like a pris'ner released from his shackles
Like a spirit set free from the tomb

Lord, You were God's precious treasure
His loved and His own perfect Son
Sent here to show me
The love of the Father
Just for love it was done
And though You were perfect and holy
You gave up Yourself willingly
You spared no expense for my pardon
You were used up and wasted for me.

CHORUS

Broken and spilled out
Just for love of me Jesus
God's most precious treasure lavished on me
You were broken and spilled out
And poured at my feet
In sweet abandon Lord
You were spilled out and used up for me
In sweet abandon let me be spilled out
And used up for Thee

-Bill George-

It is obvious that this has brought a healing of a kind to my body and my spirit, but I realize more than ever that true brokenness is a moment by moment matter and must never be taken for granted! The Psalmist declared it and I desire its reality daily.

> *"The sacrifices of God are a broken spirit; a broken and a contrite heart, O God, thou wilt not despise."* (Psalm 51:17)

A HOLY SELFIE: Life is good and very busy. God is gracious! We are blessed, daily needing time to take stock of our walk with the Lord, looking at our character, convictions, compromises and inconsistencies! Our warts and brokenness are obvious, thus we simply need time for a spiritual "defragmentation"! It is painful at first, for sin of any kind is unacceptable, demanding confession, repentance and a renewing of the mind and spirit.

Then comes the power of God's grace with the unspeakable joy of an honest confession of inability, transgressions and the "mold of iniquities" that rob one's victories. All these vestiges of sin revealed by the light of God's Word allow us to hear the sweet voice of the Holy Spirit. There is nothing like a hot bath when the grime of living in the fast lane clogs ones pores. I thank God for compassionate, caring believers who love unconditionally as we pray for one another. The treasure of God's grace indwells the "clay pots" of our flesh helping us realize that the glory is God's not ours. Therefore may we daily determine to find time in our "busy world" to seek out a quiet place for taking a spiritual "inventory"! It will indeed be a "HOLY SELFIE"! AMAZING GRACE!

Chapter Fourteen

POWER DRIVEN LIFE

G God's Work
R Righteousness Given
A Atonement Received
C Christ In Us
E Eternal Hope

GOD'S WORK

"For I will proclaim the name of the LORD, ascribe your greatness unto our GOD. The ROCK, his WORD is perfect; for all HIS ways are justice. A GOD of faithfulness and without iniquity, just and right is HE." (Deuteronomy 32:3-4)

"Come and see the WORKS of God; HE is POWERFUL IN HIS WORKS toward the children of men." (Psalm 66:5)

"...WORK out your own salvation with fear and trembling; for it is GOD who WORKS in you both to will and to WORK for his good pleasure." (Philippians 2:12-13)

RIGHTEOUSNESS GIVEN

"...believed GOD and GOD reckoned it to him as RIGHTEOUSNESS." (Genesis 15:6)

"GOD'S WORK is honor and majesty; and His RIGHTEOUSNESS endures forever". (Psalm 111:3)

"HIS name whereby HE shall be called, THE LORD OUR RIGHTEOUSNESS." (Jeremiah 23:6)

"For GOD has made JESUS CHRIST who knew no sin, to be sin in our behalf that we might be made the RIGHTEOUSNESS of GOD in HIM." (2 Corinthians 5:21)

"...WORK out your own salvation with fear and trembling for it is GOD who WORKS in you both to will and to WORK, for His good pleasure." (Philippians 2:12-13)

"But of GOD are you in CHRIST JESUS who of GOD is made unto us wisdom and RIGHTEOUSNESS and sanctification and redemption." (I Corinthians 1:30)

"For if by one man's sin death reigned by one, much more they which receive abundance of grace and of the gift of righteousness shall reign in life by one, Jesus Christ." (Romans 5:17)

ATONEMENT RECEIVED

"And the priest shall make ATONEMENT for him with the ram of the trespass offering before the LORD for his SIN which he hath done and the SIN which he hath done shall be FORGIVEN him". (Leviticus 19:22)

"...we also joy in God through our Lord Jesus Christ by whom we have now received the ATONEMENT." (Romans 5:11)

"For it is not possible that the blood of bulls and of goats should take away sins." (Hebrews 10:4)

"...I come to do thy will, O GOD taking away the first that he may establish the second. By the which we are sanctified through the offering of the body of JESUS CHRIST once for all. Every priest stands daily ministering and offering oftentimes the same sacrifices which can never take away sins. But this man JESUS after He had offered one sacrifice for sins for ever, sat down on the right hand of GOD". (Hebrews 10:8-12)

CHRIST IN US

"Whereof I am made a minister according to the dispensation of God which is given to me for you to fulfill the Word of God, even the mystery which hath been hid from ages and from generations, it now is made manifest to his saints. To whom God would make known what is the riches of the glory of this mystery

among the Gentiles which is CHRIST IN YOU THE HOPE OF GLORY; whom we preach warning every man and teaching every man in all wisdom that we may present every man perfect in Christ Jesus." (Colossians 1:25-28)

ETERNAL HOPE

"For we are saved by HOPE, but HOPE that is seen is not HOPE; for what a man sees, why doth he yet hope for? But if we HOPE for that we see not, then do we with patience wait for it. (Romans 8:24-25)

POWER DRIVEN LIFE / GRACE UPON GRACE

G GOSPEL = The death, burial and resurrection of Jesus in payment for our sin debt. Good News!

R RIGHTEOUSNESS, RECONCILIATION AND REDEMPTION = Jesus became our sin for us and gave us the gift of His righteousness reconciling and sealing us with the Holy Spirit until the day of redemption when we leave these bodies and transfer to the FATHER'S heaven.

A ATONEMENT = Christ's death on the cross and by the shedding of His blood, HE became the perfect substitute and sacrifice in full payment for our sin debt.

C COMMUNION = We come BOLDLY to the THRONE of GRACE in prayer and thanksgiving because of the cross and the resurrection.

E ENDURANCE = Jesus ENDURED his suffering empowering us that we may ENDURE all things.

The acrostic that has been used often for defining grace is God's Righteousness At Christ's Expense. The law came by Moses but grace and truth by Jesus the Christ. AGAPE LOVE IS ONE OF A KIND, UNCONDITIONAL LOVE. This GRACE-LOVE is not the norm for mankind who is given to vengeance and a return of like behavior when wronged.

Grace was not a word or reality created by men and their gods throughout the history of man. It is not a religious word but a word from the same intelligence that created gravity and the physics of the universe. This GRACE stands in judgement of the evil and criminality of mankind while at the same time loving mankind.

GRACE is not magic but an intelligent, unconditional determined love and forgiveness ordained by an intelligence that is greater than its creation and the creature, capable of thought, design and giving life.

Finally, GRACE is not a religion or philosophy but a power that can drive man to be greater than flesh and blood and empower those who receive it. Manifest by agape-love, this one of a kind unconditional LOVE which is GOD revealed.

Jesus declared,

> *"God is a Spirit and those who worship Him worship Him in Spirit and in truth." (John 4:24)*

Scriptures declare that GOD IS LOVE.

> *"No man has seen GOD at any time, the only begotten Son, [Jesus] who is in the bosom of the Father. GOD has declared HIM." (John 1:18)*

THEREFORE JESUS IS HUMANITY UNTARNISHED AND DIETY UNDIMINISHED. THUS, AS BELIEVERS WE ARE SALVAGED, DRIVEN AND SUSTAINED BY GOD'S LOVE REVEALED BY HIS AMAZING GRACE.

GRACE AMAZING / HOPE FOR THE NEEDY

Amazing GRACE shall always be my song of praise

Dancing With Grace Amazing

For it was GRACE that brought me liberty
I do not know just why He ever came to love me so
He looked beyond my faults and saw my NEED

And I shall forever lift mine eyes to Calvary
To view the cross where Jesus died for me
How marvelous the Grace that caught my falling soul
He looked beyond my faults and saw my NEED

I shall forever lift mine eyes to Calvary
To view the cross where Jesus died for me
How marvelous the Grace that caught my falling soul
He looked beyond my faults and saw my NEED
                    -Dottie Rambo-

ALL MANKIND NEEDY!

1. I need thee every hour,
Most gracious Lord.
No tender voice like thine
Can peace afford.
I need thee, oh, I need thee;
Every hour I need thee!
Oh, bless me now, my Savior;
I come to thee!

2. I need thee every hour;
Stay thou nearby.
Temptations lose their pow'r
When thou art nigh.

I need thee, oh, I need thee;
Every hour I need thee!
Oh, bless me now, my Savior;
I come to thee!

3. I need thee every hour,
In joy or pain.
Come quickly and abide,
Or life is vain.
I need thee, oh, I need thee;
Every hour I need thee!
Oh, bless me now, my Savior;
I come to thee!

4. I need thee every hour,
Most holy One.
Oh, make me thine indeed,
Thou blessed Son!
I need thee, oh, I need thee;
Every hour I need thee!
Oh, bless me now, my Savior;
I come to thee!
Text: Annie S. Hawks, 1835–1918

CONCLUSION

Self-righteous people often spend their time god talking and judging others! This repulses true believers who are struggling with what is true and nonbelievers alike. Thus believers who humbly understand GRACE are often identified with those who concern themselves with human performance and appearance rather than God's provision. Jesus defines the true believer as salt and light, both quiet witnesses to Jesus and the Gospel! The true believer understands that his/her claim to salvation is not a claim to human perfection but a declaration of NEEDINESS! A declaration of brokenness and inability that depends wholly on GOD'S RIGHTEOUSNESS. Mankind created religion to bind themselves back to their god or gods manifested by good works. Salvation is God reaching out to mankind with His Love and GRACE revealed by JESUS'S death on the cross and His bodily resurrection. JESUS Confronting our NEEDINESS through His ABUNDANT GRACE and the gift of His RIGHTEOUSNESS!   So-B-It

JESUS the Way for going / the Truth for knowing and finally / the Life for growing! John 14:6

OTHER WORKS BY DANNY GRIFFIN

- ## <u>Dancing With Broken Feet</u>
  Dealing with the pain and pressures of marriage including divorce, remarriage, blended families and more

- ## <u>Dancing With A Broken World</u>
  Danny takes his knowledge from decades of walking with the Lord and weds Biblical truth with practical living.

- ## <u>Dancing With Jesus In A Hurting World</u>
  Danny uplifts and encourages the true believer and follower of Christ to be God's ambassadorial mission in today's culture and world.

- ## <u>Dancing With Grace Amazing</u>
  The word GRACE is used 159 times in Scripture. Danny defines and explores this astounding concept.

- ## <u>Dancing With A Broken Me</u> (coming soon)
  Danny personalizes his walk with the LORD and strives to answer the question, "Who are you really, pilgrim?"

For information on how to obtain any of the above visit:
<u>http://www.SpiritualMaintenance.org/Books.html</u>

Made in the USA
Columbia, SC
24 April 2019